# Four Steps from Jesus

## A Skeptic's
## Journey to Faith

MARK JONES

# DEDICATION

For Kelly, Jim, Jonathan, Tina, Thomas,
Vladimir, Peter, Jennifer, Don, Tim, Miriam, Josh, Brittny, Craig,
Ian, Jo, Lexxi, Bob, Kelley, Kim, Read, Brian, Sean, Andy...

And anyone else who has ever wondered

# ACKNOWLEDGMENTS

The seeds for this book were sown in my mind back in college in the mid-1980s. I had a class on Christian Apologetics which is a study of the evidence for Christianity. In that class, we read a book called *The Case for Christian Theism* by A. J. Hoover. Not the most gripping title in the world, but the book had a profound impact on my life. It's perhaps outdated now, but I want to give credit where credit is due and thank Dr. Hoover for making me think so hard about this topic.

I also want to thank all my friends and family members who have asked hard questions, offered honest critique, and challenged me to tackle this intimidating, yet rewarding topic. Special thanks goes to my wife Gail for her invaluable proof-reading, suggestions, and encouragement. And finally, thanks to you for giving me a chance. I hope you're as blessed by the reading of this book as I was by the writing of it.

# CONTENTS

# PREFACE

Have you ever wondered if there's more to the universe than matter, energy, space, and time? More than animal, vegetable, and mineral? More than love and life and death and...well...more? Is there more than meets the eye? Is there any chance that having faith in something we cannot see might explain the things we can?

I've heard it said that "Gathering facts to support religion would be like gathering facts to prove that chocolate ice cream tastes better than vanilla ice cream. You can't prove preferences." [1] But is faith based on preference or on truth? Let's talk about that. It will take about an hour. I know that's a lot to ask, but this is important. Not because this book is the greatest you'll ever read. It's just that the topic we're going to discuss might be the most important you have ever considered. So, may I have an hour of your time?

# INTRODUCTION

Steps. We take them every day. Hundreds of them. Maybe thousands. Most are pretty mundane, some are fairly momentous. Think Neil Armstrong on the moon: "One small step for man, one giant leap for mankind." Think a baby's first wobbly step toward vertical motion. Think an amputee trying out a prosthesis for the very first time. Some steps change everything. I'd like to talk to you about some steps.

See, here's the deal. Many people are convinced that what we see is all there is. The world as we know it, the universe as we explore it...this is all there is to discover. Maybe you were raised that way. You have never even considered the possibility of a Creator God or a Higher Power because you've never had a reason to. Or maybe you grew up in a religious home, but somewhere along the way, you became "enlightened". You outgrew the religious boundaries of your past. You came to realize it was all just wishful thinking. Maybe you consider yourself a believer, but you're constantly fighting off the nagging doubts that keep nipping at your heels. Or maybe someone you care about deeply doesn't share your convictions, and you have no idea what to say to him or her. If any of that sounds like you, this book just might help.

Many people today have decided they simply don't believe in God--or they don't believe in God anymore. Life is no more than what we make it; evolution explains the universe in which we live; when we die, we are just food for worms. But is that true? And please don't say, "It's true for me. You have your truth, I have mine." You know life doesn't really work that way. If something is true, it's true for everybody. If it's false, it's false for everybody.

If you say that 2+2=4, and I say 2+2=3, and somebody else says 2+2=5, we can't all be right. As Ravi Zacharias put it, "Truth, by definition, excludes that which contradicts it." Nobody says truth is arbitrary when it comes to math or medicine or science. When you go to the pharmacy, you want the guys in the white coats to be very certain they are giving you exactly what's on the prescription. You want their truth to match your doctor's truth. You want the pilot flying the plane that you're on to hold rock-solid convictions concerning the laws of gravity. But when it comes to matters of faith or philosophy, some people act as if there's this *Truth Buffet* out there, and you can walk down the line and choose whatever works for you.

I understand that it is popular today to say that each of us has his own truth. That's the politically correct thing. It's much less confrontational to say, "You have your truth, I have mine," than it is to say, "I disagree with you. I believe my worldview is true, and because it's vastly contradictory to yours, that means I believe your truth is false." People do not want to say that. So they say, "To each his own."

Maybe you are less philosophical than that. You're fine with saying, "To each his own" when it comes to religion, but what you mean by that is "All religions are equal--they're equally *untrue*. If you want to believe in some ancient mythology or archaic faith system, you have every right to do that. Just leave me out of it." Perhaps you agree it's foolish to say that all truth is equal. You simply know that when it comes to religion, it's all equally *untrue*.

Can we at least agree that, as human beings, it is our duty to seek the truth? That part of our responsibility is to seek and follow that which is right and correct and beneficial? If four people are hiking together, and one insists they are heading north, another says south, another east, and another west, only one of them can be right. It's silly to say everybody has their own truth when it comes to points on the compass. Everybody can certainly have their own *opinion*, but not their own *truth*. Frankly, that's hard to communicate in the culture in which we live. We prefer gray, not black and white. Yet truth is truth.

I once read about a little boy who took his puppy to Show-N-Tell. After the kids oohed and aahed over the puppy, one of them raised his hand and asked, "Is it a boy-puppy or a girl-puppy?" The boy said, "I don't know," and then one of the other kids in the class said, "I know how we can tell. We can vote on it!" That's how many people want to determine truth: Majority vote. Yet truth is truth. Something either is true or it isn't. And whether 95% of people believe it's true, or only 5% believe it, that does not change whether it's a boy puppy or a girl puppy. Seeking truth is not a popularity contest.

That's why I believe this short book is so important: It's about a search for truth. You may be convinced that you already know the truth. I respect that. I'm pretty convinced too, and we may have vastly different opinions on what that truth looks like. Here's all I ask of you for the following four chapters. Would you at least read this with an open mind? I will not try to pound you over the head with my Bible, or back you into a corner, or trick you into believing something you know is not right. I just want to go on a journey with you, and I'm asking you to come along with me.

So here's the plan for these four brief chapters. In chapter one, I want to ask you to take one step with me. That's all, just one step: The step from being an Atheist to being an Agnostic. It's a big step, I know. But think about it. An Atheist claims the absence of God. An Agnostic claims the absence of certainty. An Agnostic does not say there is no God. Rather, he says he's not sure; he says he doesn't know for certain; he may even say it's impossible to know. If you're an Atheist right now, then at the end of chapter one, I'm certainly not going to ask you to embrace Jesus Christ as your Lord and Savior. I'm simply hoping you will say you're not sure whether there is a God or not.

The second chapter will talk about the step from being an Agnostic to being a Deist. A Deist believes there is so much design in the universe, it makes sense that there is a Designer of some sort out there somewhere. The following chapter will then consider the step from being a Deist to being a Theist: Believing in the God of the Bible. And the final chapter will discuss the step from believing in the God of the Bible to becoming a follower of Jesus. Frankly, if you look up the word Deist or Theist in the dictionary, it might define those words a little differently than I'm using them here. I simply want to use terms that you and I can get our arms around together. Who knows? You might end up like the young woman I talked to recently who checked out this material, and immediately called her friend who had given it to her. She said, "Adam, I've got great news! I'm not an Atheist, I'm an Agnostic!" I hadn't convinced her to jump into the church with both feet, but she was willing to begin a journey. That's all I'm asking you to do.

There's a story in the New Testament about a man named Paul explaining his belief in Jesus to a pagan King named Agrippa. After

Paul shared his faith journey, Agrippa said, "Do you think that in such a short time you can persuade me to be a Christian?" Paul admitted, "Short time or long, I pray to God that not only you, but all who are listening to me today may become what I am."[2]

At the end of our hour together, you may *not* be ready to accept Jesus: I get that. I simply want to show you that there is a logical progression of thought from atheism to Christianity. You do not have to check your brain at the door when you walk into a church building. Becoming a Christian does not require intellectual suicide. You may think right now that it does. I'm okay with that. I'm just hoping we can work through some of those doubts in these 60 minutes.

And one more thing. If you're a devout Atheist, I want you to know that I do not have my sights zeroed in on you as if you're a 10-point buck on the opening morning of deer season. I'm not assuming you're a hostile adversary, hell-bent on taking away my rights. I do not want to treat you like a "project" who is helpless to figure out life without me. I respect you and your right to believe whatever you choose. The fact that you are reading this book is already more than I deserve from you. At the same time, I do want to lay my cards on the table: If you're an Atheist, I want you to believe in Jesus. As a follower of Jesus, I don't hate you, oppose you, or wish you would go away. But I do believe that living a life of faith in Jesus is absolutely the best possible life--with the best possible outcome. So I want to share that with you. Believing what I do, it would be unconscionable for me to do otherwise. So, here we go. Remember, it's just an hour...

# STEP ONE:
# FROM ATHEIST TO AGNOSTIC

My wife and I had dinner one night with friends at Cracker Barrel, a down-home family restaurant. I asked the waitress, "What's the vegetable of the day?" and she replied, "Wild rice." I laughed and said, "I didn't know rice was a vegetable," and she said, "It is here!" Interesting. Does a grain become a vegetable, just because the waitress says so?

An argument over the nature of rice might not matter very much. But sometimes the discussion goes deeper. About the time the world was holding its breath over Y2K, the state of Kansas was debating whether or not "Intelligent Design" should be taught in public school classrooms as an alternative theory to evolution. That set off a firestorm of controversy over the whole idea of "truth". Stephen Jay Gould, then a professor of Geology at Harvard University, wrote an editorial in Time Magazine. He argued that religion and science should have absolutely nothing to do with one another. He said, "These two great tools of human understanding operate in...totally separate realms: science as an inquiry about the factual state of the natural world, religion as a search for spiritual meaning and ethical values." In essence, these two paths should never cross.[3] But what was he really saying? That you can search for facts, or you can search for values and spiritual meaning, but you cannot do both at the same time? That scientists have nothing to do with values, and Christians have no business dabbling in science?

I believe that if faith cannot hold up under the microscope of science, it's worthless. If faith and science contradict one another, only one of them can be right. There's no need to patronize theologians. If our faith crumbles under the weight of science, it's no good and should be declared such. The problem often comes because both sides of the debate assume they know the facts. I am not saying we can prove God through the scientific method, but science should be a tool to help us understand faith, and vice versa.

If faith is not true, then it's not really much good at explaining ethical values or the meaning of life. Truth is truth, and if we aren't operating within the realm of truth, we're just wasting our time. That's why this discussion is so important.

So as we get this journey underway, let me ask you a question. "What are the major objections to a belief in God? What causes somebody to choose to be an Atheist?" You might push back and say, "Mark, the bigger question is why you are crazy enough to believe in God?" That's a fair question, one we're going to talk about in the next three chapters. But for now, let's start with the Atheist question. Why does someone decide there is no possibility of an unseen, eternal God who created the world?

## Intellectual Barriers

Some people suggest that only Science yields truth. If it cannot be experienced by one of the five senses, it is not really truth, only conjecture. Perhaps even fantasy. Though they may never say it, deep down many people are convinced that religion is for weak-minded people who need an imaginary friend to help them sleep at night...or to make it through the day. Thomas Edison was a brilliant scientist of the 19th century. He gave his opinion on religion: "I have never seen the slightest scientific proof of the religious ideas of heaven and hell, of future life for individuals, or of a personal God. So far as religion of the day is concerned, it is a damned fake....Religion is all bunk."[4]

Many educated people feel that way, that the universe is the product of evolution--natural selection--random chance coupled with millions and millions of years. God cannot be seen, He cannot be experienced, there's simply no concrete evidence whatsoever that suggests He exists at all.

## Emotional Barriers

While some stumble over the facts as they interpret them, others reject the possibility of God because it simply feels all wrong to them. *How could there be a God when there's so much suffering in the world? Christians are a bunch of hypocrites. The idea that a loving God would send people to hell makes no sense. Religion has caused more wars than any other single factor. I've tried praying, and it just didn't do any good.* Comedian Woody Allen once said, "Not only is there no God, but try getting a plumber on the weekends."[5] In other words, my experience--or my lack of any tangible experience--tells me that religion is just wishful thinking. It's as likely as getting a clogged toilet repaired on Sunday. It's sad but true that those who are most hostile to Christianity are often those who have been hurt by somebody claiming to be a Christian. It's *not* an intellectual response to faith so much as an emotional reaction: *I've been burned one too many times, there's nothing to it.*[6]

## Lifestyle Barriers

Still further, there are those people who have chosen a way of life that they know is contrary to the teachings of God and the Bible. It's simply easier to not believe in God than to consider the implications of needing to make a life-change. They have no interest in a God who might want to interfere with their lifestyle, or their morality.

I think pride falls into this category as well. It takes humility to consider a God who is greater than mankind. That's tough for some people to even contemplate. William Barclay suggested that the heart, not the head, is the home of the Gospel [i.e. the teaching about Jesus]. It is not cleverness which shuts out the Gospel; it is pride. It is not stupidity which embraces the Gospel; it is humility.[7] It's a humbling thing--especially for a highly educated person--to embrace a belief in God when many of his or her colleagues deny that existence. The late astronomer Carl Sagan was made famous by his television documentary "Cosmos". In the opening episode of the series, he declared, "The cosmos is all that is, or ever was, or ever will be." Alex McFarland, in his book *Ten Answers for Skeptics* asked, How did he know that? Had he done an experiment? Was it a logical deduction based on the evidence? Or did he begin with the premise that God is impossible, therefore any other explanation would be better than the possibility of a Creator God?[8] That refusal to even contemplate the existence of God is fairly typical today.

Now, many people hear a discussion about the existence of God, and they immediately want to jump into a debate between creation and evolution. Either the universe evolved over millions and billions of years, or God spoke it into existence. I understand those two basic belief systems. But listen. Evolution is only one small part of a much bigger question. There is a more foundational issue than the creation/evolution controversy.

## The Question of Origins

A friend of mine said that jumping immediately into the creation vs. evolution debate is like entering a play at Scene 5. It's pretty difficult to talk intelligently about Scenes 1-4 if you missed them altogether. Try jumping into the middle of the story about Doctor Jekyll and Mister Hyde. If you knew nothing about the serum the good doctor took--attempting to eradicate evil from his heart--you would never figure out why one minute he was good and kind, and the next minute he was acting like a pit bull with rabies! You really need to start the story from the very beginning. There are some fundamental questions that have to be addressed before we ever get to either creation or evolution explaining the intricate nature of the universe.

Think of it like this. If you walk up to a pond, and you see ripples on the surface of the water--a series of concentric circles spreading outward from a single point--you would conclude that something had struck the water and started that ripple. You might even be able to trace the ripples back to the first point of contact. But what started the ripples? Maybe somebody threw a pebble into the water, maybe a stick fell out of a tree into the water, maybe a turtle surfaced from below the water, and then dove back down. You may not be sure what started the ripple, but you could see where it started.

The creation/evolution debate argues about *what* caused the ripples. Yet there are questions which precede the "origin of the ripples" discussion. Where did the pond come from? How did the water get there in the first place? Why does water even ripple? If you're looking for origins, you cannot explain the ripples on the water until you figure out the source of the water, and the explanation of ripples. An Atheist may very well believe in the Big Bang Theory. So do many Creationists. But there are questions about Origins which precede the Big Bang: How did the Big Bang come about? What caused it? What was there--or not there--before the Big Bang occurred? How did all the huge vastness of the universe spring forth out of nothing? Science is about observation. It's about forming hypotheses, carrying out experiments, evaluating the results, and drawing conclusions based on tangible evidence. Origins, however, are by nature unobservable. Nobody was there to see the beginning.

Let me ask you this: What do you remember most about your own birth? I'm not talking about photographs, or videos, or stories from your mom and dad. What do you remember most? Face it, you have no direct, conscious knowledge to draw from. You can't possibly remember. Comedian Steven Wright said, "I kept a diary since birth. I was re-reading it the other day. Day One: Still tired from the move. Day Two: Everybody talks to me like I'm an idiot!" Well, people may very well have talked to you like you were an idiot, but you don't remember that: Nobody remembers their own birth. The origin of all that exists in the universe is by very nature unobservable. What that means is that, no matter what you believe about the origin of the universe, it involves a faith decision.

**Bottom Line:** *No matter what you believe about the origin of the universe, it involves a faith decision*

As Geisler and Tureck put it, "Every religious worldview requires faith--even the worldview that says there is no God. Why? Because as limited human beings, we do not possess the type of knowledge that will provide us with absolute proof of God's existence or non-existence. Outside the knowledge of our own existence...we deal in the realm of probability.... Faith covers a gap in knowledge."[9]

We can trace things back to the very beginning, to the best of our ability, but there will always be a realm of conjecture when it comes to the Origin of the Universe because nobody was there to see it. Therefore, we gain all the knowledge we can, and then we take a step of faith. Whether you're a Creationist who believes God created the universe, or you're a sold-out Evolutionist who denies any belief in God whatsoever, it requires a step of faith. That's why I am asking you to consider being an Agnostic rather than an Atheist. Consider the possibility that

## Everything did not originate from nothing

The truth is, an Atheist can no more prove the absence of God than a Deist or Theist can prove the existence of God. We are each making a faith decision based on the available evidence. So listen: When it comes to the origin of the universe, it's not faith versus facts. It's faith versus faith. With all due respect: If you say you are 100% sure there is no God, you are claiming absolute knowledge of all things, whether you intend to say that or not. You are basically saying that there's no possibility, anywhere in the universe, that God might possibly exist.

A.J. Hoover suggested that if you had a bag of marbles and wanted to prove that there were no black marbles in it, you would have to see every marble in the bag to know for sure that none of them were black. You would have to have complete knowledge of all the marbles to prove that not even one of them was black.[10]

## Maybe God is in that one place you haven't looked

When Sherlock Holmes solves a case, he is working beyond the realm of direct experience. In other words, because he did not see the crime take place, he puts all these little pieces of evidence together and draws an ultimate conclusion. In a courtroom, it's described as *"proof beyond reasonable doubt."* That's what we're going to do in the next three chapters...talk about the scattered pieces of evidence for God. Not irrefutable evidence, but compelling evidence. Because no matter what you believe about the origin of the universe, it involves a faith decision.

When I first graduated from Bible College, I preached at a little church in western Kentucky. In this quiet farming community where we lived, a woman was abducted from the convenience store across the street from our house. She was taken away in her own car, raped and murdered, stuffed in her trunk, and brought back to the store. It was horrible--it was unbelievable. Within a couple of weeks, a man in the community was arrested. The first trial ended in a hung jury. I became acquainted with the family of the alleged killer before the second trial took place, and I found myself sitting with them during the proceedings.

There were no eyewitnesses, so the prosecution brought out

numerous pieces of evidence, none of which, by itself, *proved* anything. At the end of the trial, the prosecuting attorney and the defense attorney each were given one hour for closing arguments. The prosecuting attorney was brilliant: It was like watching a scene from a movie. He had a large bulletin board brought into the courtroom. He said, "Over the next hour, we are going to build a house." He started out with the foundation of the house. He put a long, rectangular piece of paper at the bottom of the board that listed the murder, and the victim's name. Then he began building the house one brick at a time: A piece of carpet fiber, a length of rope, some questionable trash in the garbage. I couldn't begin to remember all the different pieces of evidence now. It was over 25 years ago.

What I remember is what the attorney said after he had stacked 20-25 bricks on top of the foundation. "None of these bricks, by itself, proves the defendant committed this crime. You cannot build a house with only one brick. However, if you start with this foundation, and you build with these bricks, the only conclusion you can possibly come to is that the defendant is guilty," and he placed the roof on the house with the man's name on it.

Understand: Only one person in that courtroom had absolute, complete knowledge of the defendant's involvement in the crime. The defendant. Everybody else had to make a decision based on the evidence. I'm telling you, when the prosecuting attorney got finished, there were at least 13 people in that courtroom who were convinced the defendant was guilty. The 12 members of the jury, plus me. There may have been others, but there were at least that many. The evidence was too compelling. And so, he was sent to prison for the rest of his life.

Every day, we make decisions based on evidence. Some of those decisions are really big, most of them relatively small. Well, this is a big one. Something doesn't come from nothing. Everything doesn't just appear out of nowhere. There must be something eternal to have set all of this in motion. Naturalism says *matter* is eternal. Religion says *God* is eternal. It's a step of faith either way...because we can't know for sure.

Would you be willing to say you're not sure? Would you be willing to read on and continue the discussion? Hypothetically, let's say you are an Atheist. If you're right and I'm wrong, we will both rot in the grave. You won't have a chance to tell me, *"I told you so."* I'm sorry about that. But listen: If I am right...do you really want to risk being wrong? If not, then please read on.

# DISCUSSION QUESTIONS

1.  What were you taught growing up about the existence of the universe? Did you ever question what you were taught? Did your doubts ever lead to disagreements? What happened?

2.  Why do you think so many people struggle today to believe in God? What has been your greatest barrier to faith?

3.  Ravi Zacharias said, "Truth, by definition, excludes that which contradicts it." Do you agree? How does that influence your perspective on life?

4.  Some people believe that science and faith should have nothing to do with one another. Some scientists are insulted when faith enters the conversation, some creationists are intimidated by science. What do you think?

5.  Chapter one suggests that no matter what you believe about the origin of the universe, it involves a faith decision. Why is that? Why does it matter?

6.  If you were talking to someone who believed the polar opposite of what you believe about the origin of the universe, what would you say to him or her?

# STEP TWO
# FROM AGNOSTIC TO DEIST

A movie came out in 2009 called *Creation*. Ironically, it focused on Charles Darwin and his argument *against* the whole idea of a Creator. The movie presented Darwin as a loving husband who agonized over his theory of evolution because of his wife's strong faith. At one point in the movie, he declares, "The title of my book will be *On the Origin of Species*. I shall keep God out of it." The origin of species...without God? That's where a lot of people are today. The concept of an unseen Deity speaking the universe into existence, sculpting the planets, flinging the stars into outer space, fashioning the earth, breathing life into the first man and first woman...that all just seems like the stuff mythology is made of. I can understand that. In some ways, it seems kind of far-fetched to me too. Except that the alternative raises questions in my mind as well. That's what we are going to talk about in this chapter.

I suggested in the last chapter that no matter what you believe about the origin of the universe, it is a faith decision. Because nobody was there to see how it all began, there are certain conclusions that can only be drawn by faith. It might be faith in an eternal God, it might be faith in an eternal universe, it might be faith in everything suddenly springing forth out of nothing. But whatever you believe about the origin of all things, it involves faith.

Here, I want to take you on another journey--ask you to consider another step along the path of discovery. It's the step from being an Agnostic to being a Deist: From questioning the existence of God to considering some kind of Designer for this universe we call home. Understand, I am not an expert on all this. Huge volumes have been written about what we're going to discuss in just a few pages. I don't have enough time or knowledge to do this justice. But I do want to give you some things to think about. A suggested reading list at the end of this book offers more information if you want to continue the journey.

**Bottom Line:** *The more complex a design, the more likely a Designer*

Let's say I sat down at the table one morning to a bowl of Alpha-bits Cereal. If I glanced into my bowl, and saw an A and a T side-by-side, I might think, "Look at that, I can see a word in my cereal." If I saw R-A-T together, I might be a little more impressed. If I saw B-R-A-T together, I might show it to my wife Gail. If I saw MARK IS A BIG FAT BRAT in my bowl, I'd go find Gail and ask her why she was mad at me. She would have to be involved, there's no way that could be an accident. The more complex a design, the more likely a Designer.

Even if you put only those 17 letters "MARK IS A BIG FAT BRAT" into a box, shook them up, and then dumped them out, the likelihood of the letters falling out in that pattern--with the appropriate spaces--is incredibly unlikely. You could dump them out millions of times and you'd likely never get that exact pattern. Fill the box with other letters and start pouring, you would almost certainly never get that exact combination. No, when we see letters combined to make words, it's a pretty safe bet that somebody wrote those words. The more complex a design, the more likely a Designer.

Do you remember the old Jodie Foster movie *Contact*? She plays a fictional scientist that's part of a real-life organization called "SETI": Search for Extra-Terrestrial Intelligence. These scientists scan outer space watching and listening for a message--some unmistakable sign of intelligent life. In the movie, what did it take to capture her attention? Radio waves that appeared to have a numerical pattern: 1, 2, 3, 5, 7, 11...and so on. She recognized those were Prime Numbers, and the message contained every Prime Number from 1-101. She immediately knew these were not random radio waves from nature because the pattern was too specific. The more complex a design, the more likely a Designer.

**When it comes to our universe, the complexity of design is staggering**

There's a man in the New Testament named Paul who wrote this in Romans 1:20 (NLT) "Ever since the world was created, people have seen the earth and sky. Through everything God made, they can clearly see his invisible qualities—his eternal power and divine nature. So they have no excuse for not knowing God." In essence, *you look at the world--you look at the heavens--the majesty of all you see points to a powerful God.* Whether anybody has ever talked to you about God or not, there is an instinct in most people that says the marvels of nature are too profound to be a random accident.[11] For some, that's where Evolution comes in. For others, that's why we believe in Creation. The more complex a design, the more likely a Designer.

This actually comes down to an understanding of worldviews. Your "Worldview" is essentially the lens through which you interpret the world around you.[12] An Atheist and a Deist will evaluate the exact same information from the natural world and come to different conclusions because of their worldview. An Atheist embraces evolution: Billions of years, natural selection, and random chance gave us the universe in which we live. A Deist concludes that the vast intricacy of the universe affirms Intelligent Design of some sort.

Biologist Richard Dawkins--an outspoken Atheist--wrote, "Biology is the study of complicated things that give the *appearance* of having been designed for a purpose."[13] Because his worldview is atheism--the absence of God--he chooses to explain the "appearance of design" as the result of random chance. A Deist sees the overwhelming evidence for design and concludes there must be a Designer.

Now, before we go any further, let me explain a couple of terms to make sure we are on the same page. There are two kinds of Evolution: Micro-Evolution and Macro-Evolution. I absolutely believe in Micro-Evolution...that transformation within species has happened throughout the ages. I believe that God likely created one kind of maple tree for instance, and today we have red maples, and swamp maples, and sugar maples, and black maples which have all in a sense "evolved." God likely created one kind of canine, and today we have wolves and foxes and dogs. And not just one kind of dog: Through selective breeding, we have Great Danes and Poodles, Boxers and Dachshunds, and any number of other breeds. Some you would hardly recognize as dogs at all! I heard about one dog that was a cross between a pit bull and a Chihuahua. The owner said, "She's not much of a guard dog, but she's a vicious gossip!" This kind of variation within species is called *Micro-evolution*. Both intentional breeding and natural selection have helped species adapt.

But listen, *Macro-Evolution* is far different. Macro-Evolution says that all living things evolved from a common ancestor--from single-celled organisms. In fact, it goes back even farther than those first living cells. Somewhere in the distant past, prehistoric goo eventually led to a single-celled, living organism. In other words, the goo somehow sprang to life. That organism eventually led to a fish which led to an amphibian which led to a mammal which led to a monkey which led to a man. Evolution from one species to another.

Charles Darwin absolutely proved Micro-Evolution, variations within species. He simply made a leap then to Macro-Evolution--that one species must have led to another. See, in his experiments, finches changed, but they were still finches. Pigeons adapted, but they were still pigeons. There is abundant evidence for micro-evolution. There is no definitive proof for macro-evolution. Consider another example: We know today that when bacteria is exposed to antibiotics, certain strains of bacteria are able to adapt to the antibiotics and go on living and reproducing. Micro-Evolution. But it is still bacteria![14]

Charles Darwin said that if his theory were correct, the fossil record should demonstrate countless transitional forms, proof of "links" between the species. Even though fossils like that had not been discovered when he published *The Origin of Species* in 1859, he believed they would one day be discovered. Just the opposite has occurred in the last 150 years. Fossils continue to be found, but they are fossils of fully developed and distinct plants and animals. The Cambrian Explosion refers to a time in the fossil record when living organisms began to show up in abundance, yet the profusion of transitional forms Darwin predicted simply are not there.

When I was in High School--shortly after the Cambrian Explosion!--I had a teacher who was a staunch believer in evolution, and likely an Atheist. He commented in class one day that the skeleton of a monkey is so similar to the skeleton of a man that it proves we evolved from monkeys. My response to him was that maybe the same Creator designed both the monkey and man. Maybe God used a similar structure because that structure worked best. I didn't realize it then, but I was voicing a belief that's popular today among creation scientists: Perhaps common traits point to a common *designer* rather than a common *ancestor*. You look at paintings by Monet, Saturday Evening Post covers by Norman Rockwell, the photography of Ansel Adams...there's a stylistic similarity to each artist's work because they each designed their work in a unique way. I believe God did that too.

Dr. Owen Gingerich is a Harvard University Astronomy Professor, and the senior astronomer at the Smithsonian Observatory. He said, "A common sense and satisfying interpretation of our world suggests the designing hand of super-intelligence."[15] For the balance of this chapter, I want you to think about the design of the universe from two extreme perspectives: A big-picture view, and a close-up view. A telescopic view and a microscopic view. We'll start with the telescope.

## "Go Big or Go Home"

In the Old Testament, King David wrote in Psalm 19:1-4a (NLT) "The heavens proclaim the glory of God. The skies display his craftsmanship. Day after day they continue to speak; night after night they make him known. They speak without a sound or word; their voice is never heard. Yet their message has gone throughout the earth, and their words to all the world." The heavens, the skies, the sun, moon and stars...you just look up, and you get a sense of the wonder of the natural world.

The vastness of the universe is nothing short of astounding. As you know, our solar system is in the Milky Way Galaxy. The earth revolves around the sun. (Are you impressed with my scientific knowledge?) Well, if the earth were the size of a golf ball, the sun would be approximately 15 feet in diameter: It is massive compared to the earth. And yet, the sun is a pretty wimpy star compared to a lot of others.

One of the brightest stars in the night sky is Betelgeuse. If the earth were the size of a golf ball, the diameter of Betelgeuse would be equal to six times the height of the Empire State Building! That's pretty amazing! The star Canis Majoris is the brightest star in the night sky, literally the "Big Dog" star! If the earth were the size of a golf ball, the diameter of Canis Majoris would be the size of Mt.

Everest! There's plenty to be impressed about when it comes to the sky! But that doesn't prove a Designer.[16]

No, one of the greatest proofs for design is what's known as the Anthropic Principle. This principle essentially says the earth is perfectly designed for mankind. When it comes to planets, ours is absolutely one of a kind. Dr. Robin Collins earned his PhD in Physics from the University of Texas, and his PhD in Philosophy from the University of Notre Dame. After years of research and analysis, he became an outspoken advocate for the design of the universe. He suggests that the fine-tuning of the universe is by far the most persuasive argument for the existence of God. He often uses this illustration to talk about how perfect the earth is to sustain life.

Suppose astronauts landed on Mars and found an enclosed biosphere, similar to the domed structure which scientists built in Arizona some years ago. Suppose they found this biosphere perfectly set to sustain life: Oxygen, temperature, gravity, humidity, food, energy...everything was set perfectly. Still further, consider that if any of the systems in the biosphere were thrown off, it was designed so that that change would immediately undermine the other systems. Collins said if scientists discovered a biosphere like that on Mars, they would know intuitively that someone had taken great care to design and build that structure. There's no way they would label it an accident.[17]

Well, that's the structure of our natural world...only on a much grander scale. In the past few decades, it has become amazingly clear just how perfect our part of the universe is for sustaining life. Our earth sits 93 million miles from the sun. If we were just a few thousand miles farther from the sun, all the water on earth would be frozen. A few thousand miles closer, it would all evaporate. Oxygen makes up 21% of our atmosphere. If it were 25% of the atmosphere, for instance, fires would erupt spontaneously. If it were 15%, we would all suffocate. The moon is the perfect distance from the sun to maintain proper tidal effects without throwing off our climate. There's example after example.

In fact, Dr. Hugh Ross is an astrophysicist. He said there are 122 constants--or key factors--that make up this Anthropic Principle. The probability of any one planet having all these necessary constants without some kind of intentional design is virtually unimaginable.

Consider this: There are approximately 10,000,000,000,000,000,000, 000 planets in the universe: That's 10 trillion trillion. The probability of one planet having all 122 constants necessary to support life is one out of 1,000,000,000,000,000,000,000,000,000,000,000,000,000, 000,000,000,000,000,000,000,000,000,000,000,000,000,000,000,000, 000,000,000,000,000,000,000,000,000,000,000,000,000,000,000,000.[18] I don't know what that number is called, but it's a bunch!

If you covered the world in golf balls 10 feet deep, put a red X on one of them, and then parachuted in blind-folded and tried to pick up that one golf ball, that's the chances of a planet being as perfect as our Earth for sustaining life. And frankly, that number I just showed you is way, way, way more than the earth being covered with 10 feet of golf balls! I believe the amazing design of our universe, our galaxy, our solar system, our planet points to Intelligent Design. That's the big view--the telescopic view. Now let's dial this in and get really small with a microscopic view.

## "It's All In There"

I bought my first laptop computer "used" in about 1989. It weighed 13 pounds and had a pop-up 3.5" floppy disk drive. It was awesome! The really cool thing about it? It had a built-in hard drive. My previous desktop computer only had two 5.25" drives. No hard-drive at all. So my laptop had a built-in hard-drive. How big was it? Are you ready for this? It had a 10 megabyte hard drive! "All the memory you'll ever need" the seller told me! I have single photographs on my computer now that are far larger than that--but it sounded good at the time! The more advanced computers become, the more information they can hold.

When it comes to information storage, nothing that we come up with holds a candle to living cells. Remember in the previous chapter, we said it is not enough to talk about Creation versus Evolution: We have to go back to Origins. Where did all the "stuff" in the universe come from? Whether it evolved or not, how did matter get here? How did everything spring forth out of nothing? There are pivotal questions before we ever discuss Creation versus Evolution.

The same thing goes for the argument about whether man evolved from monkeys or not. Long before you debate man's arrival on the scene, we have the pivotal issue of where life came from in the first place.

## What is the Origin of Life?

We know that proteins are the building blocks of life. It takes about 75 amino acids to form a protein, and about 300-500 proteins to form the most basic cell. And it's not like you can just throw all that into a mixing bowl, stir it up, and out pops life--kind of like making a pot of chili. No, all those things have to line up in an exact sequence of information to form a living cell.[19] And it gets even crazier than that. Remember the example of finding a message written in my Alpha-Bits cereal? DNA doesn't use 26 letters like our alphabet does. It uses a Genetic Alphabet that only has four letters: Four nitrogen bases that are represented by the letters A, T, C, G.

These letters comprise what is known as the Four-Letter Genetic Alphabet.[20] Richard Dawkins from Oxford University--one of the most outspoken Atheists in the world--admits that the genetic code found in just the cell nucleus of a tiny amoeba is an encoded message using the Genetic Alphabet that would fill more than 30 volumes of the Encyclopedia Britannica! If you wrote out the entire genetic message which is found in a primitive amoeba, it would fill 1000 complete sets of encyclopedias! Those codes are written in order-- just like words in a book--and they must be accurate for life to be healthy and sustainable. Let me ask you something: Does that point to random chance or Intelligent Design? If it requires intelligence to write a simple sentence in my Alpha-Bits, what does the DNA coding of a living cell say about the design of the universe?

I read an article not long ago about Antony Flew, the British philosopher and author who--for years--wrote about his atheism and the foolishness of believing in God. As scientific discoveries regarding DNA and other complexities of the natural world came to light, he changed his mind and began to believe in some kind of Intelligent Design. I don't know that he became a Christian before he died, but he did write a book called, *There is a God: How the World's Most Notorious Atheist Changed His Mind.* It just makes sense to me…

*The more complex a design, the more likely a Designer*

Please understand, Charles Darwin could not have grasped the implications of DNA during his lifetime. He drew conclusions based on the information he had available to him. But with all we know today about DNA, it becomes more and more of a stretch to say this detailed information necessary for life came together by random chance. Consider this: We said proteins are the building blocks of life. DNA is the code that builds the proteins--it's like the blueprint. Therefore, proteins rely on DNA for their production. At the same time, DNA relies on proteins for its production. You simply cannot have one without the other. That being true, how could one of them have evolved before the other?[21] Give it all the time you want, there's virtually no chance they both happened to form at the same time. The implications of this are huge. Stick with me. The first living cell needed both proteins and DNA, and yet neither could have existed without the other.

Dr. Stephen Meyer earned his Master's Degree and PhD in molecular biology from Cambridge University. Not too shabby. He said it's impossible to suggest that DNA led to proteins, *or* that proteins led to DNA. You simply cannot have one without the other--you have to have both of them at the same time. He uses this example: "Suppose a guy falls into a deep hole and realizes he needs a ladder to get out. So he climbs out, goes home, gets a ladder, jumps back into the hole, and then climbs out." That's absurd: You cannot climb out of a hole, to go get a ladder, in order to get out of a hole that you can't climb out of! Meyer said that's what it's like trying to use evolution to explain proteins and DNA! There's simply too much information to imagine it all happened by chance--that proteins and DNA evolved at the same time.[22]

If you said an explosion in a print shop gave us Webster's Dictionary, that would be crazy enough. Saying proteins and DNA spontaneously formed at the same time would be like saying a second explosion--simultaneous with the first--gave us the King James Bible! The likelihood gets more and more implausible.

### *The more complex a design, the more likely a Designer*

Let me give you another quote, this one from George Wald, a Harvard University Biochemist. He said, "A scientist has no choice but to approach the origin of life through a hypothesis of spontaneous generation." In other words, a scientist must not consider the possibility of Intelligent Design, so he must find a way to embrace spontaneous generation--that life just sprung up on its own. Wald came to the conclusion that Time is the critical ingredient. He said--and read this very carefully: "Given enough time, the impossible becomes possible, the possible probable, and the probable virtually certain. One has only to wait: time itself performs the miracles."[23] Do you hear what he's saying. Life coming about on its own is impossible. However, if you give it enough time, the impossible becomes possible. Really? How does that work?

Biologist Francis Crick won the Nobel Prize for Science as a co-discoverer of the DNA molecule. He said, "Biologists must constantly keep in mind that what they see was not designed, but rather evolved." It doesn't sound to me like he's seeking truth based on evidence, but that he's looking for evidence to support a decision he's already made. When Crick came to the conclusion that life on earth could not have come about spontaneously, he came up with his "Generated Panspermia" theory: This basically says that the first living cell must have been transported to earth from a planet outside our solar system. That explains everything: It was aliens! [24]

May I be brutally honest? This is one of my greatest frustrations about the whole Creation/Evolution debate. I've been told by an Atheist friend that every time a Christian runs into a question he can't answer about science or the universe, he simply says, "God worked a miracle. That's how Christians get out of explaining the facts." In this case, a noted scientist--who absolutely refuses to consider Intelligent Design--reached a point of saying that life could not come about on its own here on earth, so it must have been transported here by intelligent life from another planet. But where did that life come from? His theory doesn't address that at all. At least Intelligent Design gets us back to a Creator. All Crick did was dodge the question of the Origin of Life by sending it into outer space.

We see it every day in art, in literature, in math, in architecture, in engineering...I believe it applies to the universe as well. *The more complex a design, the more likely a Designer.* In Lee Strobel's book, *The Case for the Creator*, he offers this analogy from Philip Gold. Using evolution to explain the universe in which we live is like saying all of this intricacy came about by rolling dice. It was all random chance, the luck of the roll. Creation on the other hand suggests the origin of the universe is more like playing a game of Scrabble. Every move is both intentional and strategic.[25] In light of what we see through the telescope and the microscope, which explanation seems more likely? I believe the complexity of the universe points to a Designer. But what sort of Designer? That's where we're heading next.

# DISCUSSION QUESTIONS

1. The creation/evolution debate often becomes intensely emotional. Why do you think this is such a volatile issue?

2. What is a worldview? How would you describe your worldview? Does your worldview ever clash with that of friends, coworkers, family members? How does a typical discussion like that play out?

3. Chapter two suggested that the more complex a design, the more likely a designer. How does that assertion impact your thinking on the universe?

4. What is the difference between micro-evolution and macro-evolution? Do you believe micro-evolution proves macro-evolution, or is it possible to have one without the other? Why is this so pivotal to the creation/evolution debate?

5. We see the suggestion/illusion of design in both the vastness of the universe, and the tiniest living organisms. What does the complexity of detail in the natural world say to you about the origin of the universe?

6. Depending on your worldview, what do you think is the strongest argument for creation or evolution? Why?

# STEP THREE:
# FROM DEIST TO THEIST

My wife Gail is very bright, very sharp mentally. At the same time, she remains electronically challenged. I'm not nearly as astute as most 9-year-olds are today when it comes to technology, but I left Gail in the dust a long time ago. Because we have a flat-screen television, a Blu-Ray player, a VCR (for all the old Disney classics we bought years ago), and surround sound, we have more than our fair share of remote controls. I'm pretty comfortable with the variety, but she doesn't see any reason to waste brain cells on all that. She just wants to know how to turn on the television, how to listen to a CD, how to watch a DVD, how to play a VHS tape.

That's why I meticulously wrote out two pages of detailed instructions on how to do each of those things: It was categorized, highlighted, the bullet points went step-by-step through each procedure; it was a thing of beauty! When I finished, I left the instructions for Gail to easily accomplish her entertainment goals. What could possibly go wrong? Well, on her first solo venture into the technological world, she called me in frustration. Forget watching a movie, she couldn't even get the television to come on. I asked her what she did. She said rather firmly, "I did exactly what you told me to. I took the large remote control, aimed it at the television, and pressed 'power.' Nothing happened." The large remote control? I had to think about that for a minute, and then it hit me. Our TV is an LG brand. She saw, "LG remote" on my instructions, grabbed the largest remote we had, and gave it her best shot! Sometimes written instructions leave something to be desired. Other times, it's more of a "user error" than a problem with the information. I'll let you decide which you believe our remote control "disconnect" was!

So far in this discussion, we have made an appeal to origins, and an appeal to design. In this chapter, the appeal is to revelation. Did God really reveal Himself to us in the Bible? Did He give us enough written information to tell us who He is and what He wants? See, many scientists today allow for some type of Intelligent Design. The intricacy of the universe in which we live--the amazing detail in the simplest living organism--seems to point to intentional order rather than random chance. Yet, the journey cannot stop there. If we are searching for Truth, it's not enough to be a Deist and believe in a Designer. That would be like my family taking off on vacation from central Indiana to Niagara Falls, getting to twelve-foot Anderson Falls just down the road, and deciding we had come far enough: "You've seen one waterfall, you've seen 'em all!" It would be like going to Ruth's Chris Steakhouse, and ordering water with lemon and a piece of dry toast. There's so much more we'd be missing out on! It would be like going on your honeymoon, and saying, "Honey, would it be all right if we just held hands tonight?" I think you get the point!

The journey of discovery cannot end with a belief in Intelligent Design. It's not enough to say that "something" out there must have helped guide the universe's progress. We need to take the next step. Who is the Designer? Which "god" created the universe? How certain can we be? Does it matter? There's a prevailing attitude today which says it doesn't matter at all. *Many roads lead to God, pick a religion and throw yourself into it. It's not a big deal what you believe as long as you're sincerely searching for God, and trying to be a good person in the process.* With all due respect, this is the Oprah Winfrey approach to religion and spirituality. Alex McFarland said, "How can anyone not like Oprah? She's nice and friendly, accepting of all people and all beliefs. A frequent theme of her program is that all religions contain truth and basically teach the same thing."[26]

And yet, all religions do not teach the same thing. Think about just a few of the major world religions.[27] Hinduism says there are 330 million gods, all believed to be an extension of one force, Brahman. Brahman is impersonal and unknowable. Hindus teach that life is based on Karma: If your life is good, it's because you are good. If it's bad, you must be bad. Hindus believe in reincarnation: After you die, you come back in a new body. If you live a good life here, you will come back with a better life next time around. If you live a bad life, your next one will be worse. A husband and wife were debating whether reincarnation is true or not. The husband said, "So you're telling me that when I die, I could come back as a worm next time?" She said, "No, I don't think you can be the same thing twice!" The goal of Hinduism is to dissolve into the oneness of Brahman.

Buddhism was founded by Siddhartha Gautama--the Buddha--some 500 years before Christ. Buddhists may be Atheists, they may believe in a god. But if they do believe in a god, he is impersonal--he cannot be known or prayed to. They do not worship Buddha; rather they seek spiritual enlightenment through meditation. The goal of Buddhism is Nirvana, ceasing to exist personally, being absorbed into the whole.

Like Christians and Jews, Muslims believe in one god--Allah--and Muhammad as his prophet. However, Allah cannot be known personally. The best a Muslim can do is to know Allah's will. Muslims respect the Bible as authentic revelation from God, but the *Qur'an* is their source of authority. They believe Jesus was a prophet of God, but not the Son of God, and certainly not divine. He was not crucified, He did not rise from the dead, He does not atone for our sins.

Frankly, many Deists don't want to worry about all those different religions: Just believe in some kind of Divine Essence--some Life Force--and call it good. It's like the "Higher Power" which is referenced in many Recovery programs. Just keep any concept of divinity very general: *To each his own.* Let me shoot straight with you: My hope is that you will at some point take the step from being a Deist who believes in some kind of Designer, to a Theist who believes in the God of the Bible. Granted, in its broadest sense, a "Theist" is anyone who believes in a personal God that can be known. I'd like to narrow the focus a little and use that term to describe someone who believes in the God of the Bible.

Take a look at these words from a man in the Bible named Isaiah, who wrote approximately 700 years before Christ. Isaiah 45:18-19, 22 (NLT), "The LORD is God, and he created the heavens and earth and put everything in place. He made the world to be lived in, not to be a place of empty chaos. 'I am the LORD,' he says, 'and there is no other. I publicly proclaim bold promises. I do not whisper obscurities in some dark corner. I would not have told the people of Israel to seek me if I could not be found. I, the LORD, speak only what is true and declare only what is right.... Let all the world look to me for salvation! For I am God; there is no other.' " That's an Old

Testament view of what Christians believe about God.

Now check out these words of the Apostle Paul from the New Testament, not long after the time of Jesus. Acts 17:24-28 (NIV), "The God who made the world and everything in it is the Lord of heaven and earth and does not live in temples built by hands. And he is not served by human hands, as if he needed anything, because he himself gives all men life and breath and everything else. From one man he made every nation of men, that they should inhabit the whole earth; and he determined the times set for them and the exact places where they should live. God did this so that men would seek him and perhaps reach out for him and find him, though he is not far from each one of us. 'For in him we live and move and have our being.' "

Revelation: God revealed Himself in a general way through the design of nature, but He revealed Himself in a specific way through His Word, the Bible. That of course begs the question: Can you believe what the Bible says about God? If so, then you can believe in the God of the Bible. If you're a Deist, but you reject the God of the Bible, then you will need to figure out which other god you believe created the universe.

I still remember the Sunday morning years ago when I tore some pages out of a Bible during a sermon. It was pretty intense. I read some verses about an explosive issue--something really controversial --and then I said, "I don't agree with that", and I tore the page out. Peoples' eyes got really big, as you might imagine. Then I turned to another place, and I read another controversial verse, and I tore that page out. I did it a third time and people were really getting nervous. "Our pastor's going straight to hell!" But then I said, "There's two things you need to know. First, this isn't a Bible!" It was actually an old textbook I had pasted some verses into. There was an audible sigh in the room. Then I said, "The truth is, a lot of people do this. They pick-and-choose the verses they like, and they tear out the pages they don't. They may not literally tear them out, but they might as well." We went on to talk about our attitude toward biblical "truth".

If the idea of a pastor tearing pages out of a Bible makes you cringe, that might say something about what you believe about the Bible. If you think it's not a big deal, that might give you a clue about your perspective as well. What we believe about the Bible says a lot about what we believe about God. So let me give you a Bottom Line, and then we'll try to unpack it.

**Bottom Line:** *The Bible cannot prove God, but it does reveal God*

There is no scientific formula or mathematical equation to make God or the Bible an open-and-shut case. But in my mind, the evidence for the Bible *persuasively* reveals God. The New Testament says in 2 Timothy 3:16-17 (NLT), "All Scripture is inspired by God and is useful to teach us what is true and to make us realize what is wrong in our lives. It corrects us when we are wrong and teaches us to do what is right. God uses it to prepare and equip his people to do every good work." That's a pretty tall order, but Christians believe the Bible does just that. So let me give you some information regarding the Bible.

**What is the Bible?**

The Bible is not a single book, it's a library of 66 books. It was written by approximately 40 different authors over a span of about 1500 years. These authors came from all different walks of life: Moses was educated in the Palace in Egypt; Peter was a fisherman; Amos, a herdsman; Joshua, a military general; Daniel was a prime minister; Luke, a doctor; Matthew, a tax collector. Paul was a rabbi, a scholar who despised Christianity at first. He ended up writing more than half of the New Testament. So much diversity. In fact, the books of the Bible were written on three different continents (Africa, Asia, and Europe) in three different languages (Hebrew, Greek, and some Aramaic).

Yet, despite all this diversity, there is an amazing thread of unity throughout the book. Namely, that God created mankind, He loves us, and He was willing to pay a tremendous price to save us from our sins. Think about it: How do you get 40 different people from 15 different centuries and three different continents to agree on anything unless it's based on truth? Granted, that doesn't prove God. But the Bible does offer a credible revelation of God--it reveals God.

Some Bible-believing people get into a debate over certain

37

specifics. For instance, were the six days of creation recorded in the first chapter of Genesis six 24-hour days, or were they six ages of time? Let's face it, the account is somewhat ambiguous. For instance, Genesis says light and darkness happened on Day One of creation, but the sun wasn't created until Day Four. Something was different in those first three days! For what it's worth, I happen to believe God created the world in six days. I believe in a relatively young earth. If God created Adam and Eve as adults--with the appearance of age--rather than as single-celled organisms--or even as infants-- why couldn't He create the universe with the appearance of age? The worldwide, catastrophic flood from Genesis 6 could account for much of the fossil record, many of the rock formations, the mountains and valleys, rivers and canyons that we see today. I do not have a problem believing God is big enough to design and create the world just as it is described in Genesis chapter one.

At the same time, I know some Bible-believing, God-loving Christians who believe the account in Genesis one is more allegorical than literal. Truthfully, I'm not sure the length of time God took to create the world is the foundational issue here. The more important issue is that, when each element of creation appeared--the planets; the sun, moon, and stars; the plants and animals; and mankind--in each instance, God spoke, and something happened. One thing did not evolve into the next, and none of it was accidental.

My Earth Science professor in college, Dr. Reuben Bullard, said, "When God created the world, He used miracle, and He used process. If He used more miracle, then He used less process. If He used less miracle, then He used more process. We do not know how much of each He used, but we know that when God created the world, He used both miracle and process." I'm good with that. That's just one example of many disputes people often have about the Bible. Yet even though we cannot necessarily resolve every dispute, I see no reason to dismiss the whole thing as ancient mythology.

It's also important to remember that the Bible contains different writing styles: History, poetry, prophecy, metaphors, parables, allegory. Most of the time, we can tell from the context which type of writing it is. But there are a few specific cases where people disagree about that too. Remember, there are some basic beliefs that are foundational to the message of the Bible, but there is room for interpretation in many areas as well.

We know that some commands in the Bible were cultural, while others were binding for all time. For instance, the Bible commands women to dress modestly. Guys struggle with lust, so we need help from women regarding how they dress. That appears to be a command which is binding for all time: Men are just as lustful today as they were 2000 years ago. However, the Bible also says women should not braid their hair. In the New Testament times, braided hair was a sign of loose morals. That appears to be a cultural command because braided hair today does not communicate anything about your morality. So the command for women to be modest seems to be binding, the command to not braid hair is cultural. That does not make the Bible any less true, it's just a matter of applying certain common-sense principles.

People often struggle with God in the Old Testament being so protective of Israel, and so vindictive against the enemies of God. The loving God of the New Testament seems totally different. Is God schizophrenic, or what? We don't have time to dig into that deeply, but here's the deal: In the big picture of the history of mankind, nothing was more important than God sending Jesus into the world. That was God's primary purpose. So when God makes life-or-death decisions about people-groups in the Old Testament, He is preparing the world for the coming of Jesus. Protecting the people of God was the most important thing at that time. Are some of the verses in the Old Testament uncomfortable? You better believe it. Did God make decisions that do not make any sense to me? Absolutely. But there's enough consistency in the Bible that I choose to trust when I don't understand. I choose to trust what I don't understand. The Bible does not prove God, but it does reveal God. Let's move on to another question.

## How did we get the Bible?

Do you remember when Dan Brown's novel *The Da Vinci Code* became such a big hit? That book and subsequent movie rocked many peoples' world because he made so many claims in there about Jesus, and how the Bible--especially the New Testament--was created. I was on an airplane one time, and sat next to a history teacher who was reading Brown's book. As we began to talk, I told him I hoped he wasn't getting his history from that novel. That began a fascinating conversation--and an on-going, on-line friendship--with a man who is seeking the truth. Yes, *The Da Vinci Code* was only a novel. But Brown claimed in the introduction--and in subsequent interviews--that what he wrote about Jesus and about the Bible was based largely on historical evidence. The basic premise of the story is that Jesus of Nazareth was a gifted teacher and a brilliant man, but certainly not the divine Son of God. He was married to Mary Magdalene and the two had a child, beginning a blood line of Christ which continues to exist today.

According to the novel--and this is the key for our purpose here--Brown said that in the 4th century the Roman Emperor Constantine, with the help of the Roman Catholic Church, squelched the truth about Jesus and Mary Magdalene. They then manipulated the New Testament documents to include teachings about Jesus' divinity and to remove any references to His humanity. It went on to assert that the New Testament was put together in a subversive way by the Council of Nicea in 325 AD, some three centuries after Christ. One of the key characters said, "The Bible did not arrive by fax from heaven. [It] is a product of man, not of God....It has evolved through countless translations, additions, and revisions. History has never had a definitive version of the book."[28] Pastor John Ortberg said *The Da Vinci Code* was one of those rare books where you would actually be dumber after reading it than you were before!

When we talk about the books of the Bible, we sometimes refer to that list as the Canon of Scripture. The word "Canon" means the norm, the standard, the rule. How and when were the Old Testament books and the New Testament books determined? The Old Testament text--the Hebrew Scriptures--were confirmed by Jewish leaders somewhere between 300-150 BC. The Greek translation of the Old Testament--known as the Septuagint--was translated no later than 150 BC and contains the 39 books of the Old Testament as we have them today. [29] The Dead Sea Scrolls--an ancient Jewish library discovered in 1947--contained portions of every Old Testament book except Esther. Long before Jesus came on the scene, the Old Testament was firmly established.

The New Testament text is obviously more central to Christians. The reality is that Jesus was a preacher, not a writer. As he went from place to place preaching, peoples' lives were changed. He made a huge impact wherever He went. In John 7:46, one of his enemies admitted: "No one ever spoke the way this man does." As Jesus' followers heard his teaching, it became part of an oral tradition. The stories and teachings were told over and over again, and sealed into the memory of the people who heard them. If you have children, you know exactly how this works. Have you ever been reading a book to one of your kids about a sleepy kitty, or some such thing, and--forget the kitty--you're the one that's exhausted? So what do you do? You try to skip a page or two. And what does he say? "You skipped a page Daddy. I want you to read all of it to me." The child can't read or write, but he knows that story word for word: It's oral tradition.

When Jesus died, his teachings were repeated by the apostles who had traveled with him, and listened to Him, and been taught by Him for three years. And when those men began to age--or be persecuted--we believe God inspired them to write this material down. And the truth is, these early writings were recognized as authentic. In fact, in 2 Peter 3:15--which was written about 67 AD-- the Apostle Peter refers to the writings of Paul as *Scripture*. The word "Scripture" refers to writings that are considered both sacred and authoritative. Granted, during the fourth century, the early Church Fathers did affirm certain Christian writings as genuine, and they denied others as phony. But it was not a whimsical decision or a close vote. They used three criteria to affirm what was already accepted as true.

## (1) Apostolic Origin

These early church leaders accepted the books that were written by the original apostles of Christ, or men who were able to interview and work alongside those followers. It is important to understand that most scholars agree: All 27 books of the New Testament were written within 20 to 60 years after Jesus died. This is huge: They were written while there were still eyewitnesses around who could challenge every word that was in them. They were being read by people who were alive when Jesus lived, and who would be able to say, "I was there--that didn't happen," if something was inaccurate.[30]

If I stood up one Sunday morning at church and said, "Ronald Reagan performed miracles, healed the sick, and walked on water," there's no way I could gather a following because so many people are around today who were alive when Reagan was. My words would not prove that Reagan was the Messiah, they would simply prove that I'm an idiot! The fact that the early Gospels of Jesus affirm His power, His teachings, His death and resurrection lends credibility to the truth.

## (2) Doctrinal Consistency

Another important criteria for the New Testament writings was a consistent doctrine. The reality is, there were books circulating in the $4^{th}$ and $5^{th}$ centuries--books that were written some 100-300 years after Christ--that were filled with contradictions and historical inaccuracies. Some of them made assertions that were directly contrary to the earlier writings. Those books lacked credibility and were never considered part of the true Bible. The books which were already well-respected were the ones that taught truth in a profound and consistent way. These spurious "gospels" are the ones which Dan Brown made such a big deal about in his novel. But they have never been recognized by the church, or by scholars of antiquity, as accurate historical accounts.

## (3) Respected Authority

Finally, the books of the New Testament which were affirmed as part of the Canon of Scripture had long been respected by the church as authoritative. They were well known among members of the Christian community. A disciple of Jesus named John wrote the Gospel of John in the New Testament; also three brief letters, and the book of Revelation. Polycarp was a disciple of John's, and Irenaeus was then a disciple of Polycarp. In the late 100's AD, Irenaeus explained that the four Gospels--Matthew, Mark, Luke and John--were so universally recognized, he referred to them in his work *"Against Heresies"* as the Four Pillars. Origen, Church Father from the early 200's AD, said: "We have approved solely what the church has recognized, which is that only the four gospels should be accepted."[31]

Former Yale Professor Williston Walker, in his book *A History of the Christian Church*, explains that the majority of what we call the New Testament today was widely acknowledged by the early 200's AD.[32]

The first church council to list the 27 books of the New Testament was the Synod of Hippo in 393 AD. But understand, the leaders at that council were not voting on which books to include, they were affirming books that were already recognized by the church. The Canon of Scripture was not so much a rambling saga through the centuries. It was a definitive collection of works gathered in the early decades following the death and resurrection of Jesus (more about that in the next chapter). While this information may be helpful in understanding how we got the Bible and how unique it is as a literary work, none of it proves the Bible is true. So we must continue to dig.

## Why do we believe the Bible?

As with the evidence for God, there is no definitive proof for the integrity of these sixty-six books of the Bible. But there are pieces of evidence that lend credibility.

## (1) Manuscript Evidence

Consider this: The two earliest biographies of Alexander the Great were written by Arrian and Plutarch more than 400 years after his death in 323 BC, yet historians consider them to be generally trustworthy.[33] Aristotle wrote his poetics around 343 BC. We have five manuscripts, the earliest from 800 AD, more than 1100 years later! And yet, scholars do not question his authenticity.[34] There are over 20,000 manuscripts of the New Testament dating back as early as 125 AD, less than 100 years after Jesus, only 30 years after John wrote the book of Revelation.[35,36]

When those early manuscripts--fragments of different lengths-- are compared to one another, experts have found there are about 184,540 words in the New Testament. There is some uncertainty with about 400 of those words. And none of the uncertainty affects any significant teaching. They are all basically spelling or grammatical issues. Evidence is strong that the New Testament is based on credible copies. It has not evolved through countless translations, additions, and revisions, as some people suggest. Josh McDowell concluded, "The Bible, compared with other ancient writings, has more manuscript evidence than any ten pieces of classic literature combined."[37]

## (2) Historical Accuracy

Archaeological discoveries continue to reinforce biblical truth. Over and over again, when secular history has questioned people, places, and events found in Scripture, new discoveries have proven the credibility of the Bible text. The Old Testament book of Joshua describes the conquest of the Holy Land by the Israelites. For centuries, skeptics insisted that the Jews gradually settled the land; there was no evidence of a conquest. However, in the last few decades, several cities have been excavated including Bethel, Debir, and Jericho. Each appears to have been furiously destroyed somewhere between 1200-1400 BC.[38]

Shortly before World War 2, Babylonian tablets were found that verified the Babylonian destruction of Jerusalem and the deportation of slaves, These events are described in the Old Testament books of Daniel, Ezra, Nehemiah.[39]

According to Time Magazine, in 1986 archaeologists found an ancient seal that belonged to Baruch, the scribe who recorded the prophecies of Jeremiah.[40] In 1993, a ninth century BC stone inscription was discovered containing the words, "House of David" and "King of Israel".[41] Also in the mid-nineties, Paul Harvey announced on his radio program that the ancient city of Ekron was discovered. An inscription stone found there included the names of kings which are listed in the book of I Samuel.[42]

In the New Testament, John chapter 5 records the story of Jesus healing an invalid by the Pool of Bethesda. John says the pool had five porticoes, or covered porches. For years, scholars thought that was inaccurate. No such pool existed. And then it was discovered and excavated. It's nearly 40 feet underground today; but guess how many porticoes it has![43]

Ancient writers have corroborated the biblical record as well. Jewish historian Flavius Josephus was born in 37 AD. He wrote about a man named Jesus who was sentenced to die by Pontius Pilate, the Roman governor. Jesus was crucified, and his followers continued in his teaching and were persecuted.[44]

Dr. Edwin Yamauchi, Professor Emeritus of History at Miami University, was asked: "Without the New Testament or other early Christian writings, what would we be able to learn about Jesus from other ancient, non-Christian sources?" Yamauchi's list of facts we know about Jesus--facts that come from ancient historical writers who were *not* followers of Christ--includes accounts of Jesus' miracles, His crucifixion during the rule of Pontius Pilate, the belief in His resurrection, the spread of the Gospel, and the fact that He was worshiped as God from the earliest times following His ministry. It's a matter of public record that history does not undermine the Bible; history underscores it. [45] And that's not all.

## (3) Fulfilled Prophecy

As I work on this chapter, I'm looking out my window at about an inch of snow. The weather forecast promised 3-5 inches, but they missed it. They tried, but they were wrong. Not terribly uncommon. Why do you suppose people gamble on everything from ballgames, to horse races, to boxing matches today? Because the result is uncertain. There's an element of surprise regarding the outcome. Yogi Berra once said, "Prediction is very hard, especially when it's about the future!"

Some scholars believe there are as many as 300 Old Testament prophecies concerning Jesus. Many are repeated, and some are more vague than others, but there are over 100 different bits of information foretelling the life and ministry of God's Holy One who was to come! The Old Testament asserts that the Savior would be born in Bethlehem, in the land of Judah. His birth would be miraculous, born to a virgin. He would be betrayed by a friend for 30 pieces of silver. The money would later be returned to the Temple, thrown down, and used to buy a potter's field where poor foreigners would be buried. He would be hung on a tree. In fact, Psalm 22 references his hands and feet being pierced, and Roman crucifixion had not even been invented yet! He would be buried in a borrowed tomb belonging to a wealthy man, and he would rise from the dead. According to the credible writings of the early Gospels, those prophecies came true in the man, Jesus of Nazareth.

Jesus once prophesied that the Temple in Jerusalem would be destroyed, and not one stone would be left upon another. His hearers were understandably skeptical; the stones in the temple were not like the bricks or blocks we often see in modern construction today. These stones were massive in size. In fact, the Temple appeared to be impregnable. Yet, in 69 AD, the Roman emperor

Vespasian gave his son Titus the dubious honor of destroying the rebellious Jews and their capital city. According to the Jewish historian Josephus whom I referenced above, Titus breached the walls of Jerusalem the next year, leading some 30,000 Roman troops into the city. Thus began a slaughter of the Jews and the destruction of the Temple in Jerusalem, just as Jesus had predicted 4 decades earlier. Josephus records that the Romans set fire to the city and the Temple, fires that were still burning a month later. The magnificent Temple was completely destroyed as the fires raged on. These fires were so hot that the gold fittings, and the gold gilding inside and out, melted and ran into the cracks between the massive stones of the Temple. The Roman soldiers later pried the stones apart to get the gold, thus fulfilling Jesus' prophecy that not one stone would be left upon another. Not just figuratively fulfilling it, but literally.[46]

Prophecies such as this may not prove the Bible is wholly true, but they lend credibility to what's recorded there. And still further, the Bible's influence attests to its authenticity.

## (4) Changed Lives

Think about it: What other book has impacted more cynics and skeptics--led more desperate people to life-transformation--than the Bible? Over and over, it has demonstrated the power to restore faith, hope, purity, peace, and love. King David wrote in Psalm 119:105, 165-166 (NLT), "Your word is a lamp to guide my feet and a light for my path....Those who love your instructions have great peace and do not stumble. I long for your rescue, LORD, so I have obeyed your commands."

Back in June of 2013, a Bible sold for $68,500 at an auction in New York City. The Bible was valuable, not because it was a Gutenberg original or a 1611 King James Version. It was valuable because of the inscription. "This book is a great source of wisdom and consolation and should be read frequently." It was given to Harriett Hamilton, and signed by Albert and Elsa Einstein. This Nobel prize winning physicist and his wife recognized the power of the Bible to impact lives.[47]

I understand, the Bible does not prove God: God cannot be proved. But the Bible does reveal God. It paints a consistent, believable, honest picture of God. It just doesn't read like a lie...or a fable or myth for that matter. If you were going to make up a story--especially thousands of years ago--you would describe the main characters as heroes, not weaklings. In ancient writings, heroes were strong, wise, victorious, larger than life. The heroes of the Bible were often weak and inconsistent, sinful, stubborn, hostile and arrogant. No, the Bible doesn't read like a lie. It reads like history. It gives details of kings, nations, time periods, and current events. It has the ring of authenticity. And because I believe the Bible, I believe in the God of the Bible.

I wish I could prove to you that the God of the Bible is the one true God. But I can't. Norm Geisler put it this way: "God has provided enough evidence in this life to convince anyone willing to believe, yet He has also left some ambiguity so as not to compel the unwilling."[48] God has provided enough evidence to convince an honest seeker, but He's also been subtle enough to avoid twisting anybody's arm. Nearly 500 years ago, Martin Luther said: "The Bible is alive, it speaks to me. The Bible has feet, it runs after me. The Bible has hands, it lays hold of me." I'm telling you, if you will let God speak to you through His Word, He will. The Bible cannot prove God, but it does reveal God.

One of my all-time favorite books is *The Hiding Place* by Corrie ten Boom. Corrie and her family were Christians in Holland prior to World War 2. When the Nazis invaded Holland, she and her family hid Jews in their home. They were eventually betrayed, captured, and sent to Ravensbruck, a notorious concentration camp. Corrie's father and sister died there, she was ultimately released. She went on to write books and tell her story all over the world.

Corrie wrote how she and her sister Betsy were able to smuggle a small portion of the Bible into the prison camp, and how they shared the good news of Jesus with any who would listen. The lice in their barracks were so bad, the guards typically left them alone. And so every night, they turned to God's Word for comfort and strength. Take a look at what she wrote:

*"Life in Ravensbruck took place on two separate levels, mutually impossible. One, the observable, external life, grew every day more horrible. The other, the life we lived with God, grew daily better, truth upon truth, glory upon glory. Sometimes I would slip the Bible from its little sack with hands that shook, so mysterious had it become to me. It was new; it had just been written. I marveled sometimes that the ink was dry. I had believed the Bible always, but*

*reading it now had nothing to do with belief. It was simply a description of the way things were--of hell and heaven, of how men act and how God acts....*

*"From morning until lights-out, whenever we were not in ranks for roll call, our Bible was the center of an ever-widening circle of help and hope. Like waifs clustered around a blazing fire, we gathered about it, holding out our hearts to its warmth and light....The blacker the night around us grew, the brighter and truer and more beautiful burned the word of God."* [49]

# DISCUSSION QUESTIONS

1. Many people believe that virtually all religions teach the same basic principles and only differ on the details. What do you think? Why?

2. If you sat down next to someone on a plane, and they asked what you thought about the Bible, what would you say? If they asked why you feel that way, what would you tell them?

3. Why do you think the Bible is so controversial?

4. Whether you believe in God and the Bible or not, there are parts of the Bible that are hard to accept. What is your greatest problem with believing the Bible as true?

5. People often say the Bible is open to interpretation. What does that mean to you?

6. Chapter three said the Bible doesn't prove God, but it does reveal God. No matter how extensive your knowledge of the Bible is (or is not), what have you learned about God from what has been written? Do you feel that information helps or hurts your openness to God?

# STEP FOUR:
# FROM THEIST TO CHRISTIAN

In the late 1970's, Lee Strobel's wife became a Christian. He was not pleased. As a legal editor for the Chicago Tribune, his life was based on facts, evidence, and the burden of proof. I once heard him say there was a sign in his office at the newspaper that read, "If your mother says she loves you, check it out!" Cynic with a capital C! When his wife decided to become a follower of Jesus, Lee was convinced that she would turn into some kind of religious prude, that she had thrown reason out the window, that his marriage was likely over. Instead, he watched her life change in a dramatic way. Her values, her character, the way she related to him and the children became so attractive, so winsome...he decided--like the sign said--to check it out.

He spent the next year and nine months investigating the claims of Christianity. He attended church, but he did much more than that. He read, he studied, he searched, he interviewed both supporters and detractors of Christianity. Basically, he did what any legal journalist would do. He sifted through evidence in a stubborn search for truth. On November 8, 1981, Lee Strobel surrendered his life to Jesus Christ and completed his journey from atheism to Christianity. He said, quote, "I discovered, in light of the torrent of evidence flowing in the direction of Christianity, that it would require more faith for me to maintain my atheism than to become a follower of Jesus." For over thirty years, Lee Strobel has devoted his life to investigating the claim that Jesus Christ is the Son of God and the Savior of the World.[50]

If by some chance you have opened up your heart and mind to the concept of Theism--believing in the God of the Bible--I'm asking you in this final chapter to consider embracing Jesus as your Lord and Savior. That's a big "Ask", I know. Even the most dedicated Christians often wrestle with doubts. In David Heller's book *Children's Letters to God*, he includes this note from a boy named Neil:

"Dear Mr. God, how do you feel about people who don't believe in you? *Somebody else* wants to know." It was signed, "A Friend." Some people hesitate to acknowledge their faith, others hesitate to acknowledge their doubt. But both perspectives are all too real.

Now, maybe you are one of those rare individuals who has never really struggled with doubt. The Gospel was presented to you at some point, it just made sense, you embraced it wholeheartedly and never looked back: There are people like that. But maybe for you, faith has been more of a stretch. Like Neil in his letter, you know "somebody else" who's not so sure. Or maybe you used to believe, but lately you're more confused than convinced. You were raised in the church, you want to believe, but nagging questions keep you awake at night. Please, don't stop searching. Don't stop seeking. This is too important.

As we begin to wrap up, we're going to take some time to investigate the claims of Jesus. If you think about it, He said some pretty outrageous things: "If you've seen me, you've seen God." "The Father and I are One." "Whoever believes in me will not perish, but have everlasting life." "God did not send me to condemn the world, but to save it." That's a lot to swallow. It's quite a stretch for a lot of people, and I can understand why. In fact, those things lead to two really important questions: (1) Did Jesus really say those things? (2) Are they true?

In the previous chapter, as we talked about the integrity of the Bible, we saw that legends about Jesus could not have sprung up over centuries of time as some have alleged. No, the teachings about Jesus being the divine Son of God--the belief that He died on the cross for our sins and was raised to life three days later--that's what the church taught in the very earliest days following the crucifixion. In fact, history points to the fact that Jesus' followers were preaching and teaching--being tortured and martyred--just months following Christ's death. Why? Because they were convinced He had risen from the dead, that He was the Lord and Savior of mankind.

The Apostle Paul wrote the book of Philippians just 2-3 decades after the crucifixion of Jesus. He included a hymn within that book which many scholars believe was already a part of early church worship. This is what it says concerning Jesus: "Though [Jesus] was God, he did not think of equality with God as something to cling to. Instead, he gave up his divine privileges; he took the humble position of a slave and was born as a human being. When he appeared in human form, he humbled himself in obedience to God and died a criminal's death on a cross. Therefore, God elevated him to the place of highest honor and gave him the name above all other names, that at the name of Jesus every knee should bow, in heaven and on earth and under the earth, and every tongue confess that Jesus Christ is Lord, to the glory of God the Father." [51] But is all that true? And if so, what are the implications for your life and mine?

As we think about the identity of Jesus, consider this. Michael Phelps is the greatest swimmer of all time. There have been amazing swimmers in the past, and there are amazing swimmers right now. Michael Phelps does not win every race in which he competes. But Michael Phelps is the greatest of all time. To prove that, I would not have to bother telling you that when Phelps was 10-years-old, he held a national record for his age group--even though that's true. I would not need to tell you that he broke the world record in the 200-meter butterfly before his 16th birthday--even though that's true. All I would need to do is show you his unprecedented 8 gold medals from the 2008 Olympics in Beijing. That achievement alone proves his dominance. You do not even have to add in his 6 gold medals from 2004, or his 4 gold and 2 silver medals from 2012. Everything rises and falls on the Beijing Olympics: *"Eight in '08"* says it all.

We are talking here about Jesus being the divine Son of God and the Savior of the World. What "says it all" for Jesus? We could talk about His profound teaching, His abundant miracles, the prophecies from the Old Testament that were fulfilled through Him. But here's the deal: Everything rises and falls on His resurrection from the dead. Just like Michael Phelps' performance in '08, Jesus' resurrection is the key. See, if Jesus made all those claims about being the Son of God and Savior of the world, and then He rose from the dead, that proves His credibility. If He said those things, but His body decomposed in the grave after His crucifixion, then He was--at best-- a nice guy and a gifted communicator...nothing more.

## Everything rises and falls on the resurrection

The Apostle Paul said in 1 Corinthians 15:3-4 (NLT), "I passed on to you *what was most important* and what had also been passed on to me. Christ died for our sins, just as the Scriptures said. He was buried, and he was raised from the dead on the third day, just as the Scriptures said." He went on to say in Verse 14, "If Christ has not been raised [from the dead], then all our preaching is useless, and your faith is useless." The resurrection of Jesus is the core belief of Christianity, so that's what we are going to talk about for the balance of this chapter. Face it, if Jesus rose from the dead, He's believable. If He didn't...well, Sunday morning church is one colossal waste of time.

Another close follower of Jesus named John wrote this in 1 John 1:1-2 (NLT), "We proclaim to you the one who existed from the beginning, whom we have heard and seen. We saw him with our own eyes and touched him with our own hands. He is the Word of life. This one who is life itself was revealed to us, and we have seen him. And now we testify and proclaim to you that he is the one who is eternal life. He was with the Father, and then he was revealed to us." Something dramatic happened to inspire John to make such a declaration.

Listen, we know the crucifixion took place. The reality that Jesus of Nazareth was killed on a cross is a sound historical fact. Any historian with an ounce of integrity believes that because of the evidence. But what about the resurrection? Why do Christians believe in that? A lot of people don't. Some have suggested that Jesus' body was stolen out of the tomb, and then the resurrection myth got started. Others said that Jesus' body was placed in a tomb, but later the disciples went to the wrong tomb, found it empty, and the resurrection was a product of their over-active imaginations. Then there's the Swoon Theory. This is not the explanation of why your wife first went out on a date with you! Some people say that Jesus just swooned on the cross--in other words, He passed out. When He was laid in a cool tomb, He later regained consciousness and came out, convincing His disciples He had risen from the dead.

J. Vernon McGee was an old-time radio preacher. He said a woman once wrote a letter to him: "Dear Brother McGee, Our preacher told us that on Easter, Jesus just swooned on the cross and the disciples nursed him back to health. What do you think?" He wrote back and said, "Dear sister, beat your preacher with a leather whip, 39 heavy strokes. Nail him to a cross and hang him in the sun for six hours. Run a spear through his heart, embalm him, and put him in an air-tight tomb for three days. Then write back and tell me what happens!"

If you've seen the movie *The Passion of the Christ*, you have a pretty good idea of what Roman crucifixion looked like. Roman soldiers were not in the habit of letting condemned criminals faint, only to be nursed back to health later on. No, death was their specialty. Jesus died on the cross, there's little doubt about that. Numerous ancient sources contain that information, even from people who were not followers of Jesus. But the question remains, why do we believe He came back from the dead? Several reasons, really.

## Eyewitness Testimony

Again, we know historically that the 27 books of the New Testament were written while eyewitnesses of Jesus were still alive. Paul said concerning Jesus in 1 Corinthians 15:5-8 (NLT), "He was seen by Peter and then by the Twelve. After that, he was seen by more than 500 of his followers at one time, most of whom are still alive, though some have died. Then he was seen by James and later by all the apostles. Last of all...I also saw him." Paul says, "Look. There are dozens--hundreds--of people still around that you can ask. They will vouch for what I'm telling you. Jesus came back to life!"

Over and over again in the Bible, small details are given to build confidence in what's been written. Now, we are used to novelists today writing fiction that's intended to sound believable. Authors make up all kinds of minor details to make the story come alive: *The smell of honeysuckle hangs in the air as the mighty hero with the bronze shield takes the fair young maiden with the hour-glass figure into his powerful arms and strokes her golden hair with his calloused hands.* Novelists often include things like time of day, season of the year, weather, what people were eating, description of facial expressions...many, many details. It gives the story the ring of authenticity.

Ancient literature did not work that way. When tales were told, they were not embellished that way. Rather, details were reserved for true stories. With that in mind, take a look at how Luke begins his New Testament account of Jesus' life. "Many people have set out to write accounts about the events that have been fulfilled among us. They used the eyewitness reports circulating among us from the early disciples. Having carefully investigated everything from the beginning, I also have decided to write a careful account..."

Luke chapter three continues: "It was now the fifteenth year of the reign of Tiberius, the Roman emperor. Pontius Pilate was governor over Judea; Herod Antipas was ruler over Galilee; his brother Philip was ruler over Iturea and Traconitis; Lysanias was ruler over Abilene. Annas and Caiaphas were the high priests. At this time a message from God came to John son of Zechariah, who was living in the wilderness." Does that sound like mythology to you, or history? If you ask me, it sounds like the evening news!

Maybe you're thinking, "The New Testament writers threw in details to trick people into thinking it was true." Well, the Bible doesn't waste words with unnecessary details either--it doesn't overdo it. When it gives specifics, there's typically a reason. For instance, the Gospel of Mark tells us that when Jesus was carrying His cross through the streets of Jerusalem, He needed some help because He was so weak from the beating He had received. It says in Mark 15:21 (NLT), "A passerby named Simon, who was from Cyrene, was coming in from the country-side just then, and the soldiers forced him to carry Jesus' cross. (Simon was the father of Alexander and Rufus.)" Why would Mark name Simon and his sons? It's not like the Bible gives tons of irrelevant details to con people into believing: "Simon, the rugged South-Paw from Cyrene-- standing 5' 11", weighing in at 175 pounds--wearing a dark brown robe with a teal blue sash--carried Jesus' cross over his left shoulder northwest through the city streets." The Bible is descriptive without being exaggerated: Details are intentional, but not excessive. Here in Mark, most scholars assume Alexander and Rufus were named because they were eyewitnesses--and they were well known. People could go to them if they wanted more information. The whole thing just has the ring of authenticity.

Another striking detail about the first eyewitnesses of the resurrection: They were women. What's the big deal about that? *Women went to the tomb first, so what? They get up earlier and work harder than men, everybody knows that.* Well, in first century times, women were considered such *unreliable* witnesses, their testimony was not admissible in court. Don't shoot the messenger on this one, I'm just relaying the facts! If the disciples were making up this story to convince people that Jesus rose from the dead, they never in the world would have said that women were the first eyewitnesses! In

55

fact, it seems like the only reason women would have been listed as witnesses at all is because they really were the first witnesses!

And think about this: James, the brother of Jesus, had been a skeptic of Jesus' ministry, and His true identity. But Paul tells us in 1 Corinthians 15 that James was a witness of Jesus after the resurrection. James later became a key leader in the church in Jerusalem, he wrote a profound letter in the New Testament, and he was eventually martyred for his faith. What changed his mind? Let me ask it this way. Do you have a brother? What would it take to convince him that you are the Son or Daughter of God? I have a brother and a sister, and I'm telling you, it would take a miracle to convince them I'm divine! Well, it took a miracle for James and Jesus too. It took the resurrection.

Still further, most of the earliest Christians were Jews. Faith in Christ began with Jews, and then spread to Gentiles throughout the Roman Empire. Listen, Jews did not worship human beings...period! Romans did. Greeks did. Faithful Jews never did! Not ever! Yet something happened that was so profound--so incredibly dramatic-- that a group of Jews decided Jesus was the divine Son of God. It's almost incomprehensible...unless you believe in the resurrection! I'm telling you, there is so much eyewitness testimony for the resurrection of Christ, seasoned attorneys have stated that--in a court of law--it would almost be an open-and-shut case. But that's not the only evidence we have. What about...

## The Empty Tomb

Jesus was nailed to a cross. A death actually took place. So, what happened to His body? If His enemies stole the body, they would have produced His rotting corpse as soon as the rumors started that He had risen from the dead. The Pharisees would have loved that! If the friends of Jesus had stolen His body just to start a rumor that He had risen from the dead, would they have really gone to their deaths for an obvious lie? Not likely. As we mentioned earlier, some have suggested that the disciples went to the wrong tomb and just assumed Jesus had risen. The tomb belonged to Joseph of Arimathea. It was a rich man's grave, probably cost him a lot of money. Did he forget which tomb he had bought? The Roman soldiers were ordered to go and guard the tomb. Do you think they went to the wrong one? When failure to obey orders meant certain death, do you think they just casually chose "any-old-tomb" to guard?

Nearly every country--and every religion with a rich history--has tombs that mark their founders. Would Jesus' followers really have abandoned the site of Jesus' burial? Not unless it no longer mattered where He was buried because He only needed that particular piece of real estate for three days! Granted, it happened nearly 2000 years ago--I get that. But the implications of an empty tomb were just as real then as they would be today. When bodies go missing, people expect to know why. They want answers. The resurrection is the only credible answer. And here's one more key piece of evidence.

## Faith Despite Persecution

The followers of Jesus were so freaked out during the time of the crucifixion, they ran from the soldiers, they hid from the religious leaders, they were cowering in fear, wondering if they were next in line for a cross. Three days later, they were proclaiming from the rooftops that Jesus was the risen Son of God. They were preaching and teaching all over Jerusalem even though they had been commanded not to. Something dramatic happened to change them! What was it? Many believe it was Jesus' resurrection from the dead!

People do not die for what they know to be a lie. Granted, people will die for a lie if they believe it's the truth. We have all read about suicide bombers who strapped explosives to their bodies because they believed it was going to enhance their experience in the afterlife. But these witnesses of the resurrection: They were being tortured and murdered because they would not stop talking about what they had seen and heard. They were not throwing their lives away for the longing of a better heavenly experience with numerous maidens. You don't get extra credit for being martyred! No, they refused to back down when they were told to recant what they had witnessed. Again, something really dramatic must have happened to convince them to stick to their story.

At the beginning of the chapter, I said everything rises and falls on the resurrection of Jesus. If He came back to life, it's safe to assume He was telling the truth. If He didn't, all bets are off. Some people like to say that Jesus was just a good teacher, and nothing more. There's even an organization called "Atheists for Jesus" that likes His teachings about the Golden Rule, loving your neighbor, even loving your enemies. They simply do not believe Jesus was the divine Son of God. But C.S. Lewis explains that Jesus really did not give us that option.[52] In the historical writings of the New Testament, Jesus claimed to be God, He said that He had come down from heaven, He insisted that He possessed power over sin and death, He forgave sins, He received peoples' worship. Lewis said, if those things were not true, and Jesus knew they were not true, that makes Him a liar. Not a good teacher, not a religious holy man, a liar. Now, if those things were not true, but Jesus thought they were true, that makes Him a lunatic. In most cases, a guy like that would be considered delusional. However, if those claims of Jesus were true, then He is the Lord. Liar, Lunatic, or Lord. Those are the three options. I believe the resurrection tells us exactly who Jesus is.

One Sunday afternoon when our family lived near Savannah, Georgia, we went to Kentucky Fried Chicken for lunch. Our arteries were running a little clean, and as a Kentucky native, I needed a taste of home! We sat down to eat, and I noticed a guy wearing a baseball cap and horn-rimmed glasses who looked really familiar. I started mentally scrolling through people from church, trying to think who he might be. About that time, my son Daniel said, "Man, did you see that guy? He looks just like Ben Affleck." I thought, "That's it, he looks like Ben Affleck, the movie star. In fact, I bet he hears that a lot--how much he looks like Ben Affleck."

I looked at him again, and I thought, "Okay, it's spooky how much he looks like Ben Affleck." But this was back during the Ben and J-Lo days, and the woman sitting across from him--though Latino--was obviously not Jennifer Lopez. However, following another subtle glance, the woman sitting next to him looked a whole lot like Jennifer Lopez! After ten minutes of whispering back and forth about the likelihood of two people looking like two movie stars, our kids walked over and asked for autographs. He said he would like to finish his meal first, but then he came over and signed their papers: Jennifer signed them too--we're on a first-name basis! I invited them to church, told them about the new church we were starting in Bluffton, South Carolina. I even gave him a recorded sermon I had about living your life on purpose for God!

But, it occurred to me later that I never said to him, "Are you *really* Ben Affleck? Could I see a photo ID? Could you quote a scene from that 'Pearl Harbor' movie, or maybe do one of those cool 'Daredevil' stunts?" I didn't ask Jennifer Lopez to sing us a song or bust a dance move to verify her identity. We said, "You know, they look a lot like Ben Affleck and Jennifer Lopez." My son Aaron said, "I heard that he has a house around here." We looked out in the parking lot and saw a Hummer: Not conclusive proof, but if it had been a 20-year-old Oldsmo-Buick, we probably would not have gone any further with our investigation! When the kids asked for autographs, this guy didn't say, "Why on earth would you want my autograph?" He said, "I'll give you one in just a minute." If you're just an average, ordinary, boring guy like me, you know it would be pretty strange to have somebody ask for your autograph. This guy acted like signing autographs was something he did every day! See, we didn't have to ask for proof of identification. We just looked at the evidence: Their looks, the nice car, the house in the area, the autographs. We examined the evidence and concluded, *That really is Ben Affleck and Jennifer Lopez.*

Listen, we will never have a face-to-face encounter with the God of the universe in this life. Until we die or Jesus comes back, there will never be conclusive, irrefutable proof that the God of the Bible is true--that Jesus rose from the dead and is the authentic Savior of mankind. When we come to the end of all the evidence we can gather, there will always be one more step of faith we have to take. But it's a step of faith, not a blind leap into total darkness! It's a decision based on credible evidence, not fairy tales.

**Bottom Line:** *Faith means taking one step beyond the evidence*

Somebody said that the same sun melts wax and hardens clay. I believe the message of Jesus is like that. Some people hear the Gospel--the Good News--and they melt. Their tough exterior softens, the message penetrates all the way to their souls. Other people hear the message, and they instantly resist. Whatever part of their heart might once have been pliable becomes hard and remote and virtually unreachable. The same message melts some, it hardens others. My prayer for you is that this book will begin a softening process. You may not be ready to embrace Jesus as your Lord and Savior, but I hope you are at least opening yourself up to the possibility of a God...and that the time may come when you will take the next step, whatever that step might be. It could be the most important step you will ever take.

A young woman named Jennifer set up an appointment with me several years ago. She came into my office with a backpack full of books and said, "Okay, I've been doing some reading." Some reading! She unpacked about 75 pounds worth of books on Christianity and other world religions--it was amazing. So she sat in my office and said, "I've decided I believe in God, but I'm not buying Jesus." I said, "That's alright," and we talked about it, talked about what she was reading. She asked some questions, I did my best to answer them. Then she asked if it was okay if she still came to our church even though she didn't believe in Jesus. I said I thought that would be just fine!

So she kept coming, and she joined a small group, and she started meeting with a woman on our staff named Kim. Jennifer always had tons of questions, and Kim did her best to answer them. Jennifer kept reading, and she kept studying, and she kept praying, and she kept coming to church. And it kept coming back to Jesus: Who is Jesus? Why Jesus? What did she really think about Jesus?

And then one day a couple of months later, she told me, "I think maybe I'm starting to believe in Jesus." And I said, "Alright," and we talked about that a little bit more. And then two or three weeks later, she called me and said, "I decided I believe in Jesus!" And I said, "Alright!" Jennifer surrendered her life to Jesus, she asked Jesus to be the Lord of her life, and Kim and I baptized her, symbolizing her cleansing and new life in Jesus. Not long after that, Jennifer came to me one day at church, her face glowing. She explained her thoughts like this: "All my life, I've talked *about* Jesus: 'This is what *Christians* believe about Jesus, this is who Jesus is *to Christians*.' But now, 'This is what *I believe* about Jesus, this is who Jesus is *to me!*' " And that decision has made all the difference in her life.

C.S. Lewis once said, "I believe in Christianity as I believe that the sun has risen: not only because I see it, but because by it I see everything else."[53] My friend, what you decide to do about Jesus is the most important decision you will ever make. So please decide very carefully. Faith is a journey. I get that. It was for my friend Jennifer, and it may be for you as well. But please keep seeking, please keep investigating. If you'd like more information, you can turn a page or two for some suggested resources to continue your search. And for what it's worth, thanks for the hour. You will never know how much it has meant to me!

# DISCUSSION QUESTIONS

1.   Mark suggested that Christianity rises or falls on the resurrection of Jesus. What does that mean? Do you agree? Why?

2.   If you watched someone die, and three days later they came back from the dead, how would that impact you? How would it affect your attitude toward them? What kinds of questions would you ask them?

3.   Have you seen the movie "The Passion of the Christ"? How did it make you feel about Jesus? Was that portrayal helpful for you in thinking about the life and ministry and compassion and strength of Jesus? Why or why not?

4.   Do you know anyone personally who has journeyed from atheism to Christianity? What kinds of things changed their mind?

5.   Where are you in your journey of faith? Skeptical? Doubtful? Hopeful? Convinced? Are you willing to continue seeking? What is a possible next step for you?

# SUGGESTED READING

*The Advancement: Keeping Faith in an Evolutionary Age*
L. Ross Bush

*I Don't Have Enough Faith to Be an Atheist*
Norman L. Geisler & Frank Turek

*Atheist Delusions: The Christian Revolution and Its Fashionable Enemies*
David Bentley Hart

*The Reason for God: Belief in an Age of Skepticism*
Timothy Keller

*Mere Christianity*
C. S. Lewis

*The New Evidence That Demands a Verdict*
Josh McDowell

*10 Answers for Skeptics*
Alex McFarland

*Confident Faith*
Mark Mittelberg

*The Case for the Creator*
*The Case for Christ*
*The Case for Faith*
Lee Strobel

*The Resurrection of the Son of God*
N.T. Wright

# ENDNOTES

[1] Norman Geisler and Frank Turek, "I Don't Have Enough Faith to Be an Atheist" (Wheaton, Illinois: Crossway, 2004), p. 22

[2] Acts chapter 26

[3] Time Magazine, August 23, 1999, p. 59

[4] Alex McFarland, "10 Answers for Skeptics" (Ventura, California: Regal, 2011), p. 18

[5] Ibid.

[6] Ibid., p. 42

[7] William Barclay, Commentary on Matthew, Volume 2, Revised Edition (Philadelphia: Westminster Press, 1975), p. 14

[8] McFarland, "10 Answers for Skeptics", p. 55

[9] Geisler and Turek, "I Don't Have Enough Faith to Be An Atheist", pp. 25-26

[10] A.J. Hoover, "The Case for Christian Theism" (Grand Rapids, Michigan: Baker Book House, 1976), p. 14

[11] Geisler and Turek, "I Don't Have Enough Faith to Be an Atheist", pp. 137ff

[12] McFarland, "10 Answers for Skeptics", p. 155

[13] Ibid., p. 57

14 Geisler and Turek, "I Don't Have Enough Faith to Be an Atheist", pp. 141

15 Lee Strobel, "The Case for the Creator" (Grand Rapids, Michigan: Zondervan, 2004), p. 128

16 These comparisons came from a talk by pastor Louie Giglio

17 Strobel, "The Case for the Creator", pp. 129-130

18 Geisler and Turek, "I Don't Have Enough Faith to Be an Atheist", p. 106

19 Strobel, "The Case for the Creator", p. 229

20 Geisler and Turek, "I Don't Have Enough Faith to Be an Atheist", p. 116

21 Ibid., p. 119

22 Strobel, "The Case for the Creator", p. 231

23 McFarland, "10 Answers for Skeptics", p. 57

24 Ibid.

25 Strobel, "The Case for the Creator", p. 219

26 McFarland, "10 Answers for Skeptics", p. 113

27 Alex McFarland offers a great summary of world religions in "10 Answers for Skeptics", Appendix 2

28 Dan Brown, "The Da Vinci Code" (New York: Anchor Books, 2003), pp. 250-251

29 Josh McDowell, "More Evidence That Demands a Verdict" (Campus Crusade Asia Limited, 1975), p. 15

[30] Ibid., p. 24

[31] Ibid., p.26

[32] Ibid., p.30

[33] Lee Strobel, "The Case for Christ" (Grand Rapids, Michigan: Zondervan, 1998), p.33

[34] Josh McDowell, "More Than a Carpenter" (Living Books, 1986), p.47

[35] Ibid., pp. 42,48

[36] Strobel, "The Case for Christ", p. 99

[37] Josh McDowell, "The New Evidence that Demands a Verdict" (Nashville: Thomas Nelson, 1999), p. 9

[38] McDowell, "More Evidence That Demands a Verdict", pp. 306-308

[39] Ibid., p.329

[40] Time Magazine, January 1995

[41] Time Magazine, December 1995

[42] Paul Harvey Radio News, July 11, 1996

[43] Strobel, "The Case for Christ", p. 99

[44] Ibid., pp.77-81

[45] Ibid., p. 87

[46] B.L. Cocherell, bibleresearch.org
http://www.bibleresearch.org/articles/a11pws.htm

[47] Fox News Science, Associated Press, June 27, 2013

[48] Geisler and Turek, "I Don't Have Enough Faith to Be An Atheist", p. 31

[49] Corrie ten Boom, "The Hiding Place" (Carmel, New York: Guideposts Associates, 1971), pp. 177-178

[50] Lee Strobel, Online video
http://www.youtube.com/watch?v=2AT_bMuFBfs

[51] Philippians 2:6-11 (New Living Translation)

[52] C.S. Lewis, "Mere Christianity" (New York: Harper One, 1952), p. 52

[53] C.S. Lewis, from a paper given to The Oxford Socratic Club, "Is Theology Poetry?"

Made in the USA
San Bernardino, CA
01 August 2016